A Four Week Devotional to Draw You Closer
To The Heart of God and Connect With His Presence

DRAW
NEAR

MONIKA KIRKLAND

Cover design and layout by Ryan Kirkland (dearryan@me.com)
Cover Photo: Alexa Mazzarello | alexamazzarello.com

For wholesale pricing and bulk orders, email hello@monikakirkland.com

"It is simply not enough to know about God.
We must know God in increasing levels of intimacy
that lift us up above all reason
and into the world of adoration and praise
and worship."

-A.W. Tozer

ABOUT THE AUTHOR

Oh, Hello. I'm Monika, I'm a wife, mama to two little girls (with another baby girl on the way!), coffee connoisseur, and lover of storytelling and writing. I have been a follower of Jesus for almost fourteen years now, but it has been in the last seven years that I have deeply encountered God's presence and love, and allowed it to transform my life from the inside out.

For years I struggled with anxiety, enslaved by my fears and insecurities. In drawing closer to God, He brought me a peace that transcends all understanding and filled me with true joy. A joy not dependent on my circumstances or other people, but a joy found in an intimate relationship with Him.

Almost three years ago, I felt God tell me that He was calling me into writing and speaking. The thought terrified me at first, but as I surrendered my will to His, my heart changed, and now I am so passionate about helping others discover the freedom, peace, and joy that can only be found in Christ. He is our refuge, our strength, our peace, and our greatest love. I pray that you would hunger for Him, and draw near to His very heart and presence.

From My Heart To Yours,

Monika Kirkland

++++++

OUTLINE

OUTLINE

INTRODUCTION

God longs to know us deeply and intimately; His desire has always been for a relationship with us. By the power of the cross and His resurrection, He defeated sin and death forever. He tore the veil in two, giving us access to His presence. It was always for us; that we might know Him and have a deeper relationship and connection with Him.

Draw near to God and He will draw near to you. - James 4:8 ESV

He is not a distant God. He is right here with us. Day in and day out. In every season, in every struggle, in every triumph: **He is right there with you.** And He longs for us to lean in and draw near to Him, *closer and closer still.*

So whether you are a new believer who has just said "YES" to God and are looking to go deeper with Him, or a long-time believer looking to connect and intentionally pursue Him, *there is a place for you here.* My prayer is that these devotionals will help you connect with God in a very real and intimate way; leading you closer towards Him and the restoration and healing that He has for you. I pray that you will both know and feel known by God; that you will feel encouraged, connected to His presence, and filled with His Spirit.

This devotional is designed as a four-week study, with five devotionals per week. I love to do devotionals and get into the word in the morning before taking on the day, but find the time that works for you! Every schedule and season of life is different, but whenever it is, try to be fully present. And if you miss a day, don't feel guilty. This isn't another item on your to-do list; it's simply a time to pursue and connect with Jesus intentionally.

Each of the devotionals ends with a prayer and response time. I've also included a recommended worship song for that day, designed to pair with the devotional. Worship is such a powerful way to align our hearts with His and to open ourselves to receive. I never feel as alive and close to God as when I am worshipping Him! Psalm 100:4 tells us that we enter His gates with thanksgiving and His courts with Praise. So whether you want to worship first, or listen while you do your response time, I highly recommend listening to the songs to help deepen your connection. I've already created a playlist to make the songs easy to access, just search "Draw Near Devotional" or Monika Kirkland on Apple Music or Spotify to access it.

So here we go, *together*, drawing nearer to the heart of God, as He, in return, draws near to us.

DAY ONE
Proud Papa

I was well into my twenties when I had a sudden revelation. One day, I was sitting outside on my back deck drinking my afternoon coffee and listening to worship when it hit me. Out of nowhere, I felt a rush of God's love for me, and I realized that **He** was proud of **me.**

You see, I had been a believer for many years at this point, but it seems I, like many others, believed that even though God loved me, He was mostly disappointed in me— like He only saw all the ways He needed to correct and discipline me and was wondering why I still wasn't getting it quite right after all these years. I thought in order to please Him or make Him proud of me, I had to be perfect. So I strived and strived to earn His approval and love, hoping that one day in Heaven He would say "well done, my good and faithful servant." What I didn't realize is that it's not about what *I do* for *Him,* it's about what He's already *done* for *me.* Grace is a beautiful gift because we don't have to earn it or strive for it. It is freely given to us because of what Jesus did on the cross. We simply have to open our hearts and receive it, to let it wash over us and transform us from the inside out.

So this revelation where I knew that God not only loves me, but is also proud of me, brought me to tears. He didn't see me as some big disappointment. That was shame, shame I had to release and let go of. I didn't have to live in fear of disappointing Him or getting it wrong. I had to believe that He chose me. That He is for me. That He beams with pride when He looks upon me.

> "And when Jesus was baptized, immediately he went up from the water, and behold, the heavens were opened to him, and he saw the spirit of God descending like a dove and coming to rest on him; and behold, a voice from heaven said, "This is my beloved son, with whom I am well pleased."
> - Matthew 3:16-17 ESV

Because of Jesus' sacrifice, when the Father looks at us, He doesn't see our sin or our shame or our past. He sees us as righteous and blameless, fully reconciled. And no amount of proving ourselves to Him could possibly make Him love us more. He looks upon us and says, "you are my daughter in whom I am well pleased!"

We hear *sermon after sermon* and sing *song after song* about His great love. And I think it's because so many of us struggle to grasp how wide and long and high and deep is His love for us. Sometime's life gets hard, or we're too distracted, and we slowly begin to forget. We tend to fall back into old patterns of striving and trying to prove ourselves because it's hard to believe that the Creator of the universe could not only **love** us but be proud of us. Shame can creep in and start to tell us otherwise, but we must cling to the truth. He fought for us, set us apart, chose us, redeemed us, and restored us. He has freed us from being slaves to sin and fear, and He longs for us to not only know but to grasp how great His love is for us.

> **"And may you have the power to understand, as all God's people should, how wide, how long, how high, and how deep his love is." - Ephesians 3:18 NLT**

So we will continue to sing of His love, to praise His name, to do whatever it takes to remind our hearts of that life-changing, profound, limitless love. The kind of love that has the power to heal us and transform us. The kind of love that once we receive, we can't help but share with the world because it has changed our lives forever. That's the kind of love that the world so desperately needs and longs for, and it begins with us. It starts with *relationship*.

++++++

Prayer: Lord, thank you that your great love for me knows no bounds. Thank you for the gift of your grace and love, that there is nothing I have to do to earn it. Thank you that you long for me to know and be known by you. Help me to open my heart and receive your love. Fill me up with the fullness of your love and your Holy Spirit today. Lord, I ask that you reveal to me any areas of my heart where shame might be lingering so that I might find new depths of healing and wholeness. In Jesus name, Amen.

Worship Song of the Day: "I See The Light (Spontaneous)" by Bethel Music & Kalley Heiligenthal, from the album "Starlight Live."

Response: Have you ever felt that you needed to strive and prove yourself to God to earn His affection? Are there any lies you've been believing about God and His nature that have kept you from encountering His love more fully? Are there any areas where shame or lies might be keeping you from receiving the depths of His love? Spend some time praying and reflecting.

_____

_____

_____

_____

_____

DAY TWO
Recognize, Remind, Repeat

I became a mother over four years ago now, and am blessed with two beautiful daughters who brighten my whole world. But one thing I didn't expect about motherhood was the influx of insecurity that came with it. Becoming a mom seemed to trigger old insecurities, and even spark a few new ones. I began to compare myself to other moms and women, and would often question my instincts and parenting. I seemed to have nailed the whole "mom guilt" thing right off the bat. I also had a really hard time trying to love and accept my postpartum body, and the world of Instagram and Pinterest seemed to confirm what I already thought: *I am less than.* My thoughts would slowly begin a downward spiral and easily consume me. The insecurities and shame quickly became a burden too heavy to bear, and it started to steal my joy. I knew this wasn't God's heart for me, and I knew I had to search for the truth amidst the barrage of lies.

> **"Let us then with confidence draw near to the throne of grace, that we may receive mercy and find grace to help in time of need." - Hebrews 4:16 ESV**

I cried out to God, and He was faithful to help me work through this insecurity and cling tightly to Him. He showed me the truth, lavished His love on me, and reminded me of who I am.

> "See what great love the Father has lavished
> on us, that we should be called children of
> God! And that is what we are!"
> - 1 John 3:1 NIV

We've all encountered insecurity at some point in our lives, and we may have to work harder to stay firm in our true identity in some seasons more than others. So, here are three things that can help ground us in truth when insecurity, guilt, or shame rear their ugly heads. I call them the three R's:

1. **RECOGNIZE** - Before you can move past what you're feeling you need to recognize and acknowledge it. Acknowledge where your guilt or insecurity is coming from. If you need help, pray and ask the Holy Spirit to reveal to you the source, or try talking to a therapist/counselor if that's an option. Maybe it's guilt over something in particular, but it could also be related to a deeper insecurity or wound you have. Whatever it is, first recognizing it and bringing it out of the darkness and into the light will help you move past it.

2. **REMIND** - Remind yourself of the truth, and break agreement with the lies that you are believing and the lie that you are not enough. Remind yourself of your identity in HIM. Remind yourself that you are a child of God, chosen and appointed! [John 15:15] If you're a mother, remind yourself that God has chosen you to raise your children,

and that you have what it takes to raise them well. Remind yourself of how loved and accepted you are by God, and let that truth sink in and encourage your soul. Living in community is also crucial here, because sometimes in our negative spiral we forget the truth or are unable to see it. Allow your community and tribe to speak life and encouragement over you, to remind you of the truth when you can't see it. It may feel tempting to live in isolation and ignore your feelings, but if you have the courage to be vulnerable and authentic with your tribe, they can help pull you out of the depths of despair in a very real way.

3. **RELEASE** - And lastly, release. Release the feelings, the insecurities, the shame, the guilt, the comparison, or whatever else over to God. I like to close my eyes, and physically open my hands and imagine it actually releasing to Him. I imagine the weight lifting off of myself, and imagine myself walking freely & lightly with Him; I thank Him that He is faithful to help us carry the load. Keep surrendering it, each day. It's not usually a "one-and-done" thing— but I assure you, it's worth it!

++++++

Prayer: Lord, thank you that you have adopted me as your son/daughter. Thank you that I no longer have to be a slave to fear and insecurity, but that I can be confident in who I am in Christ. I thank you that you give me your mercy & grace in my time of need, I only need to draw near to you. Give me the strength to surrender my insecurities and burdens to you, that I might be freer and lighter in your presence today. In Jesus Name, Amen.

Worship Song of the Day: "Lay It All Down" by Will Reagan & United Pursuit, from the album "Tell All My Friends."

Response: Have you ever felt plagued by insecurity or comparison? Or felt less than? Spend some time working on the three R's above and declaring who you are in Christ. Pray and ask God to tell you what He thinks of you. Write down what you hear and keep it somewhere where you can easily access it and read it whenever you need a reminder.

_____

_____

_____

_____

_____

_____

DAY THREE
Hearing God's Voice

One of my favorite parts of drawing close to God's presence is the increased ability to hear His voice. When I seek Him above all else, I can silence the other noise in my life and attune my spirit to listen to Him more. It is in these moments when I am praying and hear Him in return, that I feel closest to Him. I used to think that hearing from God was something other people experienced, but not me. As I've begun to encounter more of His presence and begun to hear His voice, I cannot imagine my life without it. It changes everything!

**"My sheep listen to my voice; I know them,
and they follow me."
- John 10:27-28 NIV**

The word tells us that we are His sheep and His sheep listen to His voice, but so many of us either struggle to hear from Him or doubt our ability to hear from Him at all. As we lean into His presence and seek to know Him, I want us to practice hearing His voice. That still, small voice that speaks to our spirit: *leading us, guiding us, and encouraging us.*

**"Call to me and I will answer you and tell
you great and unsearchable things you do
not know." - Jeremiah 33:3 NIV**

How do we tune in? How do we begin to hear from Him? Here are a few things that have worked for me, and I hope they will encourage you that you can hear from Him too!

1. In order to hear from God, we must first **come expectantly.** What I mean is that if we constantly believe that we don't hear from God, it will be that much harder to actually hear from Him. We must come expectantly, believing that we are His sheep and we can hear His voice. Saying and believing that you can't or won't hear from God—or fearing that it's just your own voice or thoughts— is choosing to partner with a lie. So first, believe that you can.

**"In the morning, Lord, you hear my voice;
in the morning I lay my requests before you
and wait expectantly."
- Psalm 5:3 NIV**

2. If you want to hear God's voice, you must make time to rest in His presence. Make time for stillness. Time to just be. So often the noise of the world and the chaos of our lives creates too much static to hear from God. But if we slow down, rest in His presence, and pray, we can quiet the outside noise. He is always speaking to us, but we are usually too distracted to hear or simply not paying attention. So practice meditating on His word and finding the time and space to rest.

3. Spend time reading the Word. Reading and studying scripture helps us know and understand God's nature and

character. As we begin to understand Him and His nature more, we will be able to discern when He's speaking; this will also help us to be aware that if we hear something that is not in line with His character and nature, it is not from God.

4. Begin by practicing with things you already know the answer to. For example, you can ask the Holy Spirit, "do you love me?" and wait for the response. You know God loves you, so wait to hear Him speak that truth to your Spirit. It's not usually an audible voice, but a soft impression on your heart. Doing this little exercise helps you recognize His voice and how He speaks to you.

5. And finally, stay connected to your community and home church. Staying connected to the body of Christ helps us hear God for both ourselves and others, that we might encourage and build up His church. God can use other people to speak into our lives or to confirm something we believe we're hearing from Him. We can lean on each other for understanding, wisdom, and discernment on what we are hearing from God. We are not meant to walk alone!

Be patient with yourself as you to learn to hear the voice of God in your life. We are His children, and we can be confident that He is with us and He is always speaking!

++++++

Prayer: Lord, thank you that you are always speaking to me. I pray that you would open my eyes to see you and my ears to hear you. Help me to quiet the noise in my life so that I can hear you speaking. I come before you expectantly, believing that you will speak to me today. In Jesus name, Amen.

Worship Song of the Day: "Spirit of the Living God" by Vertical Worship, from the album "Vertical Worship."

Response: Do you hear from God regularly? Do you believe you are able to hear from Him? Take a few minutes to silence your mind, and ask God to speak to you. Write down anything that you hear, and try not to be discouraged if you don't hear anything. This takes practice, and we will continue to practice it throughout the coming weeks.

_____

_____

_____

_____

_____

DAY FOUR
Follow The Breadcrumbs

"'For I know the plans I have for you' says the LORD, 'plans to prosper you and not to harm you, plans to give you hope and a future" - Jeremiah 29:11 NIV

Do you ever feel like you want to have your life all figured out? To know exactly how to get from point A to point B, and have a clear and direct path to follow?

While I cherish adventure and moments of spontaneity, I typically love having a plan. I prefer to have clear direction and know which steps to take to get to where I want to go.

But this last year and a half have been such a wild adventure with the Lord, with me often having to trust Him to give me insight and clarity with each step I take. There have been so many amazing moments where God has spoken to me and through me. Where He has encouraged me and guided me both through prayer and also through other people speaking into my life. I am so grateful for that; grateful that He has given me more insight into the call and plan He has for me. However, sometimes, if I'm honest, it can also create this internal pressure that I need to "make it all happen." And before I know it I'm running full speed ahead trying to take charge and figure it all out.

13

One week my mind and spirit were a little restless as I was marinating on some conversations I'd had, and some words that were spoken over me that I didn't quite understand. I trusted God, *and yet* I also wanted to have everything figured out and know exactly where He was leading me. I went to bed one night with my thoughts spinning and my heart longing for clarity. I was seeking Him and praying through it, but I still felt a bit restless as I went to bed.

And then that night I had a beautiful dream, a dream that encouraged my heart so much. In the dream I encountered God, and He spoke to me and said, "You don't have to have it all figured out yet, you just need to keep following the breadcrumbs."

That was it. That's all He said, but it was exactly what I needed to hear. Simple, yet profound wisdom. I woke up feeling the presence of the Holy Spirit, and I felt peace rush over me. I just need to keep following the breadcrumbs, I thought. It's not up to me to figure it all out. I will certainly play my part, but it's not on me. We're in this together. **The weight and pressure are lifted off of me when I remember it's all in partnership with *Him*.** God doesn't only care about the final destination or end result; He cares about the process. About the journey. We don't need to have all the answers or even know the exact destination, and what a wonderful gift that is. How *freeing*.

We don't need to live in fear of getting it wrong or going off-track, because He is faithful to gently pull us back in the right direction and work it all together for good. He will guide our steps. **We can walk in complete trust and complete peace.** We may not always have all the answers, but we can rest in knowing that He's a good, *truthworthy* Father.

> **"And the peace of God, which transcends all understanding, will guard your hearts and your minds in Christ Jesus."**
> **- Philippians 4:7 NIV**

God has a plan and purpose for our lives, and He is always laying out breadcrumbs. We simply need to keep following Him and trust that He will continue to lay them out for us. He won't abandon us or leave us helpless! Yes, we certainly have our part to play, and there may be times where we have to step out in faith, but we don't need to stress or strive— **we just need to follow the breadcrumbs.**

Keep following. Keeping drawing closer. He is Faithful. He is trustworthy. He is who He says He is and He will do what He says He will do!

++++++

Prayer: Lord, thank you that you have great plans for me and have crafted me for a purpose. Help me to seek first you and your kingdom, and trust that you will lead the way for me. Help give me the wisdom and discernment to hear your voice, and to recognize the breadcrumbs you are leaving out for me. Fill me with your peace that transcends all understanding, and help give me the courage and boldness to step out in faith when the time comes. In Jesus Name, Amen.

Worship Song of the Day: "Take Courage" by Bethel Music & Kristene DiMarco from the album "Starlight Live."

Response: Ask God to reveal a glimpse of His purpose for you. Pray that throughout the coming weeks He will move in your life and leave breadcrumbs for you. Ask Him to speak to you through His word, through prayer, through others, and even through your dreams. Journal and write out a few specific prayers so that we can look back and see how God has been faithful.

DAY FIVE
Relentless Pursuit

If you've ever lost someone close to you, you know the pain, the grief, the questions, and the what-ifs that tend to follow. An emotional roller coaster with its many twists and turns.

I've lost two people in my family; their lives cut too short as they lost their battle with addiction. Most recently, my oldest brother, only in his thirties. Shock and then the grief, as you receive the phone call you feared was inevitable unless something changed.

As I was processing and grieving and looking through photos, I stumbled upon a message from my brother that I had since forgotten about. Six months before he passed, he reached out to me because God had been speaking to him through his dreams. My brother was a professed atheist, but he wrote to me because even though he had more questions than answers, he said he couldn't deny that God was speaking to him. God had told him in a dream that he was His son and that He loved him. His heart softened as God continued to speak and pursue him. As I read through that message and reflected on our conversations, my eyes welled up with tears, because that right there is the goodness of our God and savior! He will stop at nothing. He will leave the 99 and go after the 1! There is no wall He won't kick down, no lie He won't tear down, in His relentless pursuit for us. His love for us is so great that even in the depths and throws of addiction He will come to you to claim you as His son or daughter and tell you how loved you are! That goodness, that faithfulness, that *reckless love* overwhelms my heart, and I can't help but praise His name!

And to give me that message, dated only six months before, was a gift to me as well. It brought me peace and reminded me that His grace and love knows **no bounds.** He hadn't forgotten or forsaken my brother. He relentlessly pursued him, came to him in visions and dreams and made sure he knew he was loved.

> "What man among you, if he has a hundred sheep and has lost one of them, does not leave the ninety-nine in the open pasture and go after the one which is lost until he finds it? "When he has found it, he lays it on his shoulders, rejoicing. "And when he comes home, he calls together his friends and his neighbors, saying to them, 'Rejoice with me, for I have found my sheep which was lost!' - Luke 15: 4-6 NIV.

His love is our firm foundation. May we be sons and daughters who grow roots deep down into that love. May we love Him and others with that kind of pure, unconditional love: *a love that overwhelms and restores.*

++++++

Prayer: Lord, I am overwhelmed by your goodness! Thank you for your reckless love and endless pursuit of us. I thank you that you love us, even at our lowest, that you never stop. I lift up prayers for those caught in the bondage of addiction, that they will break those chains and walk in complete freedom! I thank you that you are a God of restoration and that you are making all things new. Help me to be rooted in your love, today and everyday. In Jesus name, amen!

Worship Song of the Day: "Reckless Love" by Passion (Featuring Melodie Malone), from the album "Whole Heart (Live)."

Response: In what big or small ways has God been pursuing you and showing you how much He loves you? Reflect and remember any moments in your life and story where you felt overwhelmed by His goodness and faithfulness, and celebrate them today. Lift up prayers for those people in your life who still need to encounter His love. Write down their names and entrust them to Him.

_____

_____

_____

_____

DAY SIX
Saying "Yes" To God

It was over two years ago now, I was sitting at a women's retreat when I felt God tell me He was calling me to writing and speaking. At first, I was like "who *me?!* I just had a baby! I barely have time to take a shower let alone write and speak!" The thought of it sounded terrifying. But slowly, over time, He kept nudging my stubborn heart, and I started to notice a shift. I started to want what He wanted. I began to lay aside my fear and doubt and trust His plans for my life! I didn't know the when or the how or anything at all, but my little heart whispered back, "Lord, have your way with me."

Slowly I started to see Him move in amazing ways! I was sitting on the couch one evening when I happened to go on Instagram. I saw that Bianca Olthoff, a writer and speaker I loved, was doing an internship program called A Seat At The Table. I thought it was an awesome idea and I "liked" the post and scrolled past— not even considering that it could be a good fit for me. I immediately I felt the Holy Spirit tell me to apply. Again, I had so many questions… what would that look like? What would I do for childcare? Would I be the oldest one there?! But I could not deny that God was clearly telling me to apply. And it was what my heart longed for: *a seat at the table.* A place to connect and glean from those who have gone before me! I decided that instead of focusing on all the ways it wouldn't work, to see all the ways that it would!

I followed the link and filled out my application right then and there. I knew if I waited too long I would talk myself out of it or lose my nerve. I acted in obedience and applied in faith, and left the rest in God's hands!

> **"Say a quiet yes to God, and he'll be there in no time."**
> **- James 4:8 MSG**

Several weeks later I went through two rounds of interviews, and then I received the news that I had gotten the internship! I was blown away by God's faithfulness. That summer turned out to be such an incredible season of growth and transformation in my life! I would not be where I am today without that experience. Sometimes it's the things that scare us the most that produce the most fruit and growth in our lives!

When we trust God and act in obedience, amazing things happen. We don't need to focus on all the ways it won't work— we need to trust God that it will!

> **"And we know that in all things God works for the good of those who love him, who have been called according to his purpose."**
> **- Romans 8:28 NIV**

God has a plan and purpose for our lives, and as we steward our relationship with Him, **He** will steward our call. When we seek His presence and trust His timing and process: He will be faithful. It may be scary, we may have to push past our fears and insecurities, but when we say "YES!" to God— there is nothing He can't do!

++++++

Prayer: Lord, thank you that you love me and have created me for a divine purpose. Help me to say "YES" to you, even when it scares me. Please quiet the noise in my life so that I can hear your voice speaking to my heart. Give me wisdom and discernment to see where you are moving in my life, and where you are leading me. Help me to prefer you above all else! Increase my faith Lord, that I will trust you for the things that feel impossible! In Jesus Name, Amen.

Worship Song of the Day: "Yes and Amen" by Chris Tomlin, from the album "Never Lose Sight."

Response: Is there something you've felt God calling you to that scares you? What does it look like to say "yes" to God in this season? Tell God about any fears or insecurities that may be holding you back, and release them to Him.

_____

_____

_____

DAY SEVEN
Perfectly Imperfect

One of the earliest memories I have is when I was about five years old. I was in the kitchen when my dad was cooking, and as I walked past the stove, my arm caught the handle of the pot, knocking it over, and spilling baked beans all over the floor. I immediately began to cry. It was such a small thing, and clearly an accident, but it was the first of a series of moments in my life where I felt like a failure. I hated that I upset him; that I messed up.

Right then, that moment, this spirit of perfectionism got a hold of my heart. I would aim to be perfect. To never mess up. To get it right. In school, I would push myself to take advanced classes and get straight A's. To make my teachers and my parents proud. I craved approval and validation and thought if I could be good enough, then I would be loved and accepted.

I pushed myself so hard on the outside because on the inside I did not know my worth. My thoughts were toxic— my inner dialogue was full of me talking down to myself for not being smart enough, pretty enough, thin enough, talented enough, creative enough. I became a total slave to perfectionism. My insecurities and fear began spiraling out of control, producing anxiety in my life. I was always seeking validation, because I thought if other people would like me and accept me, maybe I would like and accept myself. If someone told me I was smart, maybe I was. If someone told me I looked beautiful, then perhaps I could start to believe it was true. But this way of living creates a dysfunctional cycle, where you live by praise and die by criticism. And it's never ever enough. Like a drug, you keep coming back for *more, more, more*.

Perfectionism and comparison tend to go hand in hand. We compare our lives with others and are left feeling like we don't quite measure up. Comparison is the doorway to envy: longing for what others have rather than being grateful for all that we've been blessed with. It skews our perspective and disconnects us from God's heart for us.

"A heart at peace gives life to the body, but envy rots the bones." - Proverbs 14:30 NIV

If we're so busy looking at everyone else, we forget what is right before us! As the saying goes, "comparison is the thief of joy"— because that's what it does. It robs us of the precious gifts of joy and contentment.

It has been a long road to healing, of reminding myself who I am in Christ. As I draw close to Him and His heart, I can begin to see myself and others as He sees us: redeemed and justified through Christ. **I am enough because He is enough.** Instead of comparing myself to others, I can celebrate them because we are all significant and unique and wonderfully made in His image.

"Even before he made the world, God loved us and chose us in Christ to be holy and without fault in his eyes. God decided in advance to adopt us into his own family by bringing us to himself through Jesus Christ. This is what he wanted to do, and it gave him great pleasure. So we praise God for the glorious grace he has poured out on us who belong to his dear Son."
- Ephesians 1:4-6 NLT

God's perfect love is not dependent on us being perfect. We have been adopted as His sons & daughters, and we have to remember our true identity comes from Him. We must free ourselves from the fear of man, and receive our validation from Christ alone. In doing this, we release our fear and shame of not measuring up or being good enough and walk in complete freedom and peace.

++++++

Prayer: Lord, thank you that I am enough because you are enough. Help me to align my heart and mind with yours. Give me new eyes to see myself and other people as you see us. I renounce perfectionism, people-pleasing, striving, and the anxiety they bring. I declare that I am no longer a slave: I am free. In Jesus Name, Amen.

Worship Song of the Day: "No Longer Slaves (live)" by Bethel Music & Jonathan And Melissa Helser, from the album "We Will Not Be Shaken (Live) [Deluxe Edition]"

Response: Do you struggle with perfectionism or comparison? Ask God to show you how He sees you. Ask Him to help you identify any lies you believe about yourself, so you can partner with the truth and be who He has called you to be.

DAY EIGHT
Present In The Mess

It was a long day that turned into a long night. I was tired and in need of some serious "me time" after a day of meeting everyone else's needs. My soul was crying out for something life-giving, something to help pull me out of my funk. But if I'm honest, all I wanted was to put my feet up, make myself a bowl of ice cream, and binge watch a show on Netflix.

Mama was **done**.

I was ready to tune out, check out, and distract myself from my life. To shut off my brain and just "veg." Don't we all get to that point sometimes?

Why is it so hard to stay present right there in the middle of the mess? In the middle of the ugly, hard parts of life? In the middle of our weaknesses? It is there where we create space for Jesus to show up. If we *check out* then we *miss out* on His ability to be all that we need. Our little distractions may temporarily relieve, but they can never **restore**.

> "But he said to me, 'My grace is sufficient for you, for my power is made perfect in weakness.' Therefore I will boast all the more gladly about my weaknesses, so that

Christ's power may rest on me."
- 2 Corinthians 12:9 NIV

We need to lean in and be present in these moments, even (and especially) when we want to escape. I'm not saying you can never watch TV or relax, but check the condition of your heart. Are you giving your soul the breath of fresh air that it needs to truly thrive? We need to get real and raw, opening ourselves up to God; inviting Him into the messy and vulnerable parts of our lives and stories. Drawing close and drinking of His living water.

> **"Jesus answered, 'Everyone who drinks this water will be thirsty again, but whoever drinks the water I give them will never thirst. Indeed, the water I give them will become in them a spring of water welling up to eternal life.'"**
> **- John 4:13-14 NIV**

If we can be honest with ourselves and with God, and pour our hearts out to Him, He will provide the true comfort and restoration our souls are craving. We won't find it anywhere else.

> **"Trust in him at all times, you people; pour out your hearts to him, for God is our refuge"**
> **- Psalm 62:8 NIV**

++++++

Prayer: Lord, thank you that you are my comfort and my place of refuge. My soul cries out to you, and I thank you that you hear my cries. Let me not settle for any artificial substitutions, but let me come directly to the source of life. I thank you that in my weakness you are made strong. Help me to be present and to show up even on the messy, hard days. In Jesus Name, Amen.

Worship Song of the Day: "My Soul Longs for You" by Jesus Culture, from the album "Come Away (Live)"

Response: Do you ever try to "check out" or look for distractions on hard days? Get honest with God and confess anything or any person you turn to in place of Him. Ask Him to be your strength on your weakest of days and your place of refuge.

_____

_____

_____

_____

_____

DAY NINE
Bloom Where You Are Planted

Let's set the scene, shall we? We zoom into a young, ambitious, twenty-something with stars in her eyes and great hope for her future— but slowly, as we zoom out, we see her empty expression and see that she is confined in a small, dark cubicle; wasting away on spreadsheet after spreadsheet. Desperate for something that gave her life, something that utilized her gifts and creativity. She sat there, day after day, wishing away her current reality and ready to move on to bigger, better things.

Ah yes, the big reveal: *that girl was me.* And yes, I know it's a bit dramatic. I tend to be just a tad bit dramatic. Just ask my friends.

But that's what it felt like, five days a week, at my "big girl" job (as I called it). I was grateful for it, as it helped provide for my husband and me. And I loved the people I worked with; they were all wonderful and kind. But I couldn't shake this nagging hollowness I felt each day in that dark, cold office staring at my computer screen. I longed to go into acting and to write full time. I was anxious and ready for our move to California; ready for a change of scenery, ready to escape the office and go on an adventure.

What I wish I could go back and tell my younger self is this: "bloom where you are planted." Dreaming big is important, it gives us hope and perseverance. And I am so incredibly grateful for the dreams God put on my heart. Dreams that ultimately led us to where we are today. However, with that said, I also think it is incredibly important to embrace our current reality. There is much to learn, much to grow from, and so much to pour out— but if we are so consumed with ending one season and rushing on to the next, how can we possibly be open to all God has to show us?

> **"Whatever you do, work at it with all your heart, as working for the Lord, not for human masters" - Colossians 3:23-24 NIV**

Looking back: there were so many opportunities I missed, friendships I missed out on, growth that could've happened. That girl, sitting in her cubicle, had already checked out. Mentally and emotionally. She knew she was moving to California to start her new life and new adventure there. So even though she had a whole year there, at that job, in that community— she was so busy looking ahead that she forgot to be present where she was. She forgot to bloom.

> **"Give your entire attention to what God is doing right now, and don't get worked up about what may or may not happen tomorrow." - Matthew 6:34 MSG**

Rather than feeling like we are "waiting" for our life to begin, what if we gave our entire attention and focus to what God is doing in our lives right now? **In the present. This day.** Not waiting for "someday" when we graduate school, or find a husband, or start a family. Or "someday" when we get our dream job and find success. Or next year, next month, next week. Whatever that thing is that you're waiting for.

Because the truth is: this is it. This is our life. It has already begun.

And it's a choice that we can make today and every day— a choice to bloom. To embrace our current season and live in the present moment. To walk with God and work with God. To allow Him to lead us. To draw so close to Him that His presence is what carries us from one season to the next. That we hear His voice and ask Him to reveal how we can learn and grow right here, right in the season we're in.

> **"Jesus said, 'No procrastination. No backward looks. You can't put God's kingdom off till tomorrow. Seize the day.'" - Luke 9:62 MSG**

Seize **this** day so that you can truly bloom where ever you are planted. This season, as dry and barren as it may seem, may actually hold something truly beautiful for you.

Don't be so busy looking ahead that you miss it.

++++++

Prayer: Lord, help me to live right here in the present with you. I pray that I would experience all that you have for me in this season of my life. Help me continue to learn and grow and to draw near to you in the process. Thank you for all the ways you are working things together for my good— help me to trust you every step of the way. In Jesus Name, Amen.

Worship Song of the Day: "Oceans (Where feet may fail)" by Hillsong United, from the album "Zion."

Response: How is the condition of your heart in this season? Are you living in the present? Ask God to reveal to you any ways you can learn and grow throughout this time. Entrust Him with your future, so that you can live in the present.

_____

_____

_____

_____

_____

DAY TEN
Freely & Lightly

There is a place I go, down by the harbor, a little cove carved right into the side of a cliff, where the waves crash loudly into the rocks, and the shore disappears at high tide. It has become *my place*. The place I go to meet with the Lord and soak in His goodness and mercy. The place I go when my soul needs rest and restoration. The place I go where I can sit and be still in His presence, and trust that He will meet me there.

I find peace there when the world around me seems to be moving at lightning speed, and I'm scrambling to keep up. I've gone there in seasons of mourning and seasons of great joy. I go there when I need to think, when I need to pray, when I want to meditate on His word, or when I need stillness.

One thing I've noticed in my years of doing ministry is that so many suffer from burnout. In our efforts to serve God and others, we forget to take the time to rest. To allow ourselves time to care for our hearts and souls, and connect with ourselves and our families. Before long, the weight of it comes crashing down on us, and we are burned out on religion. Sometimes it's physical burnout and exhaustion, other times it's spiritual and emotional burnout. Feelings of isolation, discouragement, and even bitterness come pouring in; sometimes leading people to walk away from their church, ministry, or their faith altogether.

> "Are you tired? Worn out? Burned out on
> religion? Come to me. Get away with me, and
> you'll recover your life. I'll show you how to
> take a real rest. Walk with me and work with
> me—watch how I do it. Learn the unforced
> rhythms of grace. I won't lay anything heavy or
> ill-fitting on you. Keep company with me, and
> you'll learn to live freely and lightly."
> - Matthew 11:28-30 MSG

The type of relationship and abundant life God is calling us into is not heavy and ill-fitting: it is free and light. We must walk so closely with Him that we can learn how He does it; that we can learn His unforced rhythms of grace. We will only discover it in company with Him. The one who brings real rest and renewal. The one who recharges our batteries and fills our cups so that we can give and serve out of the overflow.

> "Abide in me, and I in you. As the branch cannot
> bear fruit by itself, unless it abides in the vine,
> neither can you, unless you abide in me. I am
> the vine; you are the branches. Whoever abides
> in me and I in him, it is he that bears much
> fruit, for apart from me you can do nothing."
> - John 15: 1-5 ESV

We cannot bear fruit unless we abide in Him. The Greek word for abide is *meno*, and it means "to stay, to remain." We must stay connected and in His presence if we want to produce fruit. Just as the branch is connected to the vine, and receives all of its nutrients, water, and minerals—everything it needs to thrive—from the vine, we too must stay connected to God so that we may thrive. We are entirely dependent upon him. And yet even though we know this, it is so easy to get caught in our routines, caught in the doing, and forget to abide in Him. We forget our complete dependence on Him and begin to think we are strong enough to do it ourselves, leading to a cycle of perpetual burnout.

We must hold steadfast to Jesus so that we can learn to truly live freely and lightly. We must trust Him, trust His word, and continue to rest in Him. As we begin to honor our priorities, we will learn how to set healthy boundaries and know when to say *no*, and then we can finally begin to break the cycle of burnout.

Remain in His love— this is the way that leads to life, to fruitfulness, to freedom.

++++++

Prayer: Lord, thank you that you are my life source. You are all I need. Help me to abide in you always; that I may bask in your presence and goodness, and be filled with your Holy Spirit. Show me how to live freely and lightly and recover my life. Help me not to get so caught up in the doing that I forget to remain in your love. I release any burnout and stress to you and pray that you will give rest to my weary soul. Help me to live and work in partnership with you. In Jesus Name, Amen.

Worship Song of the Day: "Abide (Breathe Me In)" by Ryan Kirkland, from the album "Wanderer." Yes, this is my husband. He is amazing.

Response: What are some of your warning signs when you experience emotional, spiritual, physical, or relational burnout? Are there any areas in your life where you need to adjust your priorities to allow you time to rest in His presence? Do you have a place of refuge where you can go to feed your soul and encounter God? Maybe it's somewhere in nature, or a particular corner in your home, or your church. Wherever it is, try to set aside time this week to go there and abide in Him.

_____

_____

_____

_____

_____

DAY ELEVEN
He's Got You

There I stood, over a year ago now, staring out at the Pacific Ocean and crying out to God, "Lord, show me the way. Tell me what to do, and I'll do it." It was like I was standing at a crossroads, wondering which direction to take. I didn't know what the right decision was. I didn't know which path to take. I didn't know **what to do.**

I prayed for clarity. Of course, the easiest response would have been a specific and clear "yes" or "no" answer, but God wasn't giving me a direct response. And instead of revealing to me which way to go, He reminded me, through scripture and wise counsel, *what to do when you don't know what to do.* What to do when you are in a season of waiting on God. When you are waiting for an answer or waiting for clarity. Maybe you are waiting for a spouse, a child, a job, or waiting to be healed. Whatever it is, God gently reminds us what to do and what His will for that moment is. No matter the circumstance.

So if you are in a season where you are crying out to God for answers, here are five reminders of God's will and steps you can take today.

1. Love Him and Love others. We know that God's will and desire for us, simply put, is to love Him and love others. It is so easy to get stuck in our heads and overcomplicate this, letting our mind and thoughts spiral out of control, creating anxiety in us. But if you are loving God with your whole heart and loving others as you love yourself, then you are living out God's will for your life. Don't be so consumed with figuring out which path to take that you forget to put your whole heart into these two commandments.

> "Jesus replied: 'Love the Lord your God with all your heart and with all your soul and with all your mind.' This is the first and greatest commandment. And the second is like it: 'Love your neighbor as yourself.'" - Matthew 22:37-40 NIV

2. "Rejoice always, pray continually, and give thanks in all circumstances" [1 Thessalonians 5:16-18]. Scripture tells us that this is God's will for us every situation. If you're asking God for clarity and not getting a direct answer, this is one clear picture of what you can do, today. If we can be people who actually practice this, not just in theory, but in actuality, we set ourselves up to receive all that God has for us. Of course, it can be so hard to live this out, especially in dark times— but our Joy is found in the Lord, and we can rejoice in Him. If you are in a season where you feel like you have nothing to be thankful for, look around you and give thanks for every little thing. Start with giving thanks for the breath in your lungs and the shoes on your feet and go from there. Let's be Christ followers who are well-versed in the art of gratitude, not just when things go our way.

3. Live out what trust looks like. In my situation, God's plan was being carefully orchestrated and executed all around me, even though I couldn't see it. He needed me to trust Him and trust the process. And rather than say "trust me," He revealed to me what trust looks like in action. And what that looks like is praying, rejoicing, and giving thanks for all He has done and all He is about to do (as discussed above). What trust does not look like is wandering around anxiously, fearful, and full of doubt that God will keep His promises. If you want to trust Him but are struggling with doubt and fear, worship is a great way to create space in your mind and heart for the peace of the spirit.

4. Be proactive. He will reveal the plans He has for you, but He also wants us to be proactive. God does not want us to sit idly by, twiddling our thumbs. You can be proactive. If you don't know what step to take, then take the next best step. God is a good Father, who works all things together for our good. We can't let the fear of making the wrong choice prevent us from being proactive. Fear is a powerful emotion, but ultimately, even if you get it wrong, you can trust that God will set your path straight and work it together for your good and His glory.

> "Trust in the Lord with all your heart, and do not lean on your own understanding. In all your ways acknowledge him, and he will make straight your paths." - Proverbs 3:5-6 ESV

5. Lastly, seek wise counsel. If you don't have a mentor, seek out a Pastor or wise friend or family member. Tell them your circumstance and your plans; ask them to pray *for you* and *with you.*

Usually, the situations we don't want to ask for advice with are the ones we need it the most. Sometimes we are afraid we will hear an answer we don't want, but we need to have courage and be open, as it can save us so much heartache and pain later on.

"The way of fools seems right to them, but the wise listen to advice." - Proverbs 12:15 NIV

Know that you know that you know you are loved by a God who sees you and is for you. So no matter what you're facing, no matter which step you take, even if you are walking in the unknown— **He's got you.**

++++++

Prayer: Lord, thank you that you are with me, even in the midst of unknowns and unanswered questions. I rejoice and give thanks to you for your great love and sacrifice for me! Help me to trust in you with all my heart, and believe in your faithfulness. I thank you for how you are moving in my life and pray that you help me to walk in victory today and every day! In Jesus name, Amen.

Worship Song of the Day: "Fear Not" by Kristene DiMarco, from the album "Where His Light Was"

Response: Have you ever felt discouraged when you didn't receive a clear answer from God? How can you cling tighter to God even in the midst of unknowns? Do you feel led to take any of these steps today?

_____

_____

_____

_____

_____

_____

DAY TWELVE
Made Whole

I struggled a lot in my early teen years. I was a broken girl, from a broken home, trying to navigate all of my teenage emotions and feelings. I was desperately insecure and trying to figure out where I fit in this world. I had so much pain inside— pain I didn't know how to express. So I kept it all bottled up, and thought if I could convince myself and everyone else that I was fine, I would be. But pain has a way of seeping out of us. I struggled with insomnia, depression, and eating disorders. My home life was a mess, and I didn't have a safe place to turn to.

It was there in my brokenness, in my pain, that God came and rescued me. He plucked me out of the darkness and adopted me into His royal family. I love this quote, "Waiting to come to the Lord when you get your life cleaned up is like waiting to go to the ER when you stop bleeding. He doesn't love some future version of you; He loves us in our mess."

He loves us right there in our mess, in our brokenness! But He also doesn't want us to stay that way. He takes our broken halves and makes us whole. He brings healing and transformation from the inside out, by the power of His Holy Spirit.

"I am sure of this, that he who started a good work in you will carry it on to completion until the day of Christ Jesus."
- Philippians 1:6 CSB

God doesn't just settle for us believing and going to heaven when we die. He wants to bring His kingdom **now**, on earth as it is in heaven.

He is faithful to bring healing and restore hope. He is faithful to shed light on the darkest parts of us. Faithful to work all things together for our good. Faithful to pour out His blessings, that we might overcome all obstacles and schemes from the enemy that hold us back. Bringing us closer to Him and closer to our true identity in Him.

"It is for freedom that Christ has set us free. Stand firm, then, and do not let yourselves be burdened again by a yoke of slavery."
- Galatians 5:1 NIV

We are no longer slaves. We can live and walk in healing and wholeness. We don't need to strive *for* victory, because the battle has already been won. Instead, we live from *victory* knowing and believing that we have been set free, set apart, restored, and redeemed.

++++++

Prayer: Lord, thank you that you have set me free and redeemed me, and that I am more than a conqueror through you. Thank you that you are restoring all things. Let me live from that place of victory and walk in complete freedom. Continue your good work in me, and fill me with abundant faith throughout the process. In Jesus Name, Amen.

Worship Song of the Day: "More Than Conquerers" by Rend Collective, from the album "Good News."

Response: Do you feel free? Is there an area of your life where you want to experience more freedom in Christ? Pray and ask God what work He wants to do in you today so that you can experience wholeness and freedom. Ask Him to fill you with the power of the Holy Spirit, that you may experience further healing today.

_____

_____

_____

_____

_____

_____

DAY THIRTEEN
When It's Time To Let Go

It feels like a lifetime ago, like a completely different person. But there I was… only 21, with stars in my eyes and big dreams of taking the acting world by storm. I had worked hard and saved hard, and moved all the way across the country from Orlando to Los Angeles with my husband, Ryan. He was always so supportive and really believed in me. We both craved adventure, and we were excited to start our new life in California. So off we went in our little Toyota Corolla on our three-day road trip to the City of Angels.

I had dreamed of becoming an actress since I was five years old. I did plays at summer camp and in school and loved the art of storytelling. I learned through movies, I learned about life and family and friendship. I'm a deep feeler: their stories became my story. And I couldn't wait to tell people's stories through film and TV.

I had big dreams, like many young actresses before me. I had potential. I had talent. I had drive. I loved the Lord and thought I was "called" to act. And while I do believe God gives us the dreams in our heart, I never actually consulted God on the matter of whether or not I should be an actor. I prayed, sure, but it was a one-way conversation, where I mostly just asked God to "bless" my career. I was so committed to achieving this dream. I didn't want anyone (especially God) to tell me it wasn't the right path.

So there I was. Desperate to "make it." Desperate to prove the nay-sayers wrong (YES I KNOW THE ODDS AND I DON'T CARE, I AM MEANT FOR THIS!)— I got a manager, and began to audition. And audition. And audition.

As someone who already struggled with a spirit of rejection, the worst thing I could do for my soul was go into a career where you receive rejection every. single. day. I knew, theoretically, that it wasn't personal, but it sure felt personal. My heart ached. I grew exhausted and isolated and struggled with anxiety. Maybe I wasn't cut out for this life after all. I had so much pressure (from myself) to succeed at this thing I thought I was meant for.

After two years of striving and aching and borderline low-grade depression, my husband and I decided to move an hour south of LA to Orange County to be closer to our church family. I knew it was the right next step, and yet I didn't want to do it. But God had asked me to trust Him with this, to trust Him with my dream. So I decided to take a step back from pursuing acting, and begin a family with the love of my life. Soon after we were pregnant with my daughter, Eveleigh.

See, with acting, I had a narrow vision for my life. I was so focused on my desire to act, that I forgot that I had other passions and desires too. Through taking a step back from acting, I learned that I also loved writing and photography and ministry and leading.

"Many are the plans in a person's heart, but it is the LORD's purpose that prevails."
- Proverbs 19:21 NIV

God needed me to trust Him with that dream so that He could reveal **His** dreams for me. To create space for Him to reveal His divine calling and purpose for my life. And it wasn't always easy, but the best thing I've ever done was laying down my dreams and desires and saying "Lord, have your way. Not my will but yours be done."

"I will instruct you and teach you in the way you should go; I will counsel you with my loving eye on you." - Psalm 32:8 NIV

It's amazing what can happen when you are willing to let go of what you thought your life would look like. What passions are revealed and what opportunities come your way when you partner with God on **His** calling for your life. I never want to do it any other way. How much more fulfilling, purposeful, and organic can it be than when you partner with God?!

And now, in this season, I am seeing the fruit of laying that dream down. I am partnering with God on this new God-breathed vision for my life. I am still using my love of storytelling, except now it's God's story I'm telling. I am walking with Him every step of this journey. I am inviting Him into it, letting Him guide me and lead me. I am staying close to Him and tuning in so that I can hear His voice and guidance.

What are we holding onto that the Lord is gently telling us, "let go and trust me?"

It may be the hardest thing you've ever done, but I promise you, it will be worth it.

"Let God have your life;
He can do more with it than you can."
- Dwight L. Moody

++++++

Prayer: Lord, thank you that you have great plans for me. Help me to tune in and hear your voice, and to have the courage to go where you lead. I surrender my plans and desires to you and ask that you would have your way with me. Reveal to me anything I have been holding onto that you are calling me to let go of, and give me the faith to do so. In Jesus Name, Amen.

Worship Song of the Day: "Called Me Higher" by All Sons & Daughters, from the album "The All Sons & Daughters Collection."

Response: What dreams has God put on your heart? Is there anything you need to say "no" to so that you can say "yes" to His dreams for you? Ask Him how can you can partner with Him in the work He is doing in your life. Write down anything you hear and continue to seek His direction.

DAY FOURTEEN
Trust Fall

I remember the day I accepted Christ into my life. I was fourteen and had been attending a local youth group. I had been
going for months on the promise of "cute boys," but something about the accepting and loving environment kept me
coming back. I had a lot of preconceived notions about what
"church people" were like, but something felt different there. I
felt welcomed. Even with my punk rock clothes and dark eye-
liner, I felt accepted. I wasn't quite sure about all the "Jesus"
talk— but I kept going back week after week. I didn't realize
that each week, being there and hearing the music and the
messages, was slowly planting seeds in my life and softening
my heart to God's love. One night, the youth pastor invited
us into a personal relationship with Jesus, and I said "yes" to
God for the first time.

My life with God wasn't an immediate, radical change, but a
subtle shift and transformation over many years of continuing
to follow Him. I had to slowly learn to trust Him, to trust
that His intentions towards me were good. Up until that
point, I had a general mistrust of others, especially authority
figures. I held on very tightly to all control in my life, because
for so long I had believed that the only one who could take
care of me was me. It was a slow process of healing and surrendering and learning to trust in His faithfulness. Of slowly
beginning to hand over different areas of my life and will to

Him.

> "Teach me to do your will, for you are my
> God. May your gracious Spirit lead me
> forward on a firm footing."
> - Psalm 143:10 NLT

God never forces Himself on us; He patiently waits for us to come to Him and give Him authority over our lives. Areas of unsurrendered will, the parts of our hearts and lives that we refuse to give to Him, only keep us from fully experiencing and encountering His presence. Just as unconfessed sin can be a block between God and us, causing us to run away from Him in shame, so too are the things we have a tight-fisted grip on and refuse to release. Those things in our lives that we struggle to fully surrender and trust Him with distance us from His presence and keep us from the abundant life He has for us.

We must trust Him and surrender every part of our lives to Him: our past, present, and future. Our fears, our plans, our marriages, our families, our parenting, our relationships, our finances. Everything. We surrender it to Him and ask that His will, not ours, be done. It is in this that our faith and trust grows, as we learn to submit to His great authority.

Have you ever seen that video of the "trust fall" exercise, where the girl's sister is ready to catch her from behind, but instead she falls forward and crashes face first into the ground? That's what it's like when we misplace our trust or lean on our own understanding. God is right there, ready and waiting to catch us, but we're heading the wrong direction and putting our trust in the wrong things. And then before we know it we're falling flat on our faces. But we can choose to lean on Him and trust that He will never fail us. We can choose complete surrender.

> **"It is better to trust in the LORD than to put confidence in man." - Psalm 118: 8 KJV**

What usually keeps us from full surrender and submission? Fear. Fear tells us everything will fall apart if we let go. Fear tells us not to trust God or anyone else for that matter. Fear tells us we're on our own. Fear overwhelms us and creates anxiety about the future. Fear puts our faith in the wrong people and things. Fear stunts our growth and paralyzes us.

But we can rest assured that God's perfect love casts out all fear, and we can renounce our fears in the name of Jesus. We allow Him to replace our fear with *faith* as we entrust every part of our lives and hearts to Him. Once we do this, we are finally able to walk in complete trust and freedom, fully surrendered to our Father.

> **"There is no room in love for fear. Well-formed love banishes fear. Since fear is crippling, a fearful life—fear of death, fear**

of judgment—is one not yet fully formed in love." - 1 John 4:18 MSG

God wants to be Lord over all. He doesn't want pieces of us, and He doesn't want to share us. He wants all that we have and all that we are. He wants to sit on the throne of our lives. And if we come humbly before Him, submitting to His will and recognizing our complete dependence on Him, He will lift us up.

"Humble yourselves in the sight of the Lord, and He shall lift you up." - James 4:10 KJV

++++++

Prayer: Lord, thank you that your perfect love casts out my fear. Help me to believe that you are worthy of my trust, that your intentions towards me are good, and that I can lean on you. I submit all that I have and all that I am to you, bringing it under your authority and Lordship. Help me to humble myself before you, that you might lift me up. In Jesus Name, Amen.

Worship Song of the Day: "Lord Over All (Live)" by Kari Jobe, from the album "Majestic."

Response: Do you have a hard time letting go and surrendering to God? Are there any fears that you need to recognize and renounce so that you can trust Him and submit to Him? Ask God to reveal to you any unsurrendered will you might have in your life. Open the palms of your hands and imagine yourself physically releasing it and entrusting it to Him.

_____

_____

_____

_____

_____

_____

DAY FIFTEEN
Changing The Narrative

A story all moms can relate to, I'm sure: my sweet baby girl, up from midnight until 3 a.m., not going back to sleep despite our best efforts. She was sleeping in our room at the time, so both my husband and I were awake with her, trying desperately to get her to go back to sleep. But she was wide awake. Playing, cooing, babbling to us. Finally, around 3 a.m. we get her back to sleep, only to be woken just three hours later at 6 a.m. to start our day.

We were tired. Irritable. Cranky. And I knew, at that moment, that we had a choice. The choice to let that exhaustion dictate our day. To go through the day frustrated and irritated, gritting our teeth and baring it, anxiously awaiting naptime and bedtime. **Or.... or** we could choose to change the narrative. We could choose to shift the atmosphere of our home and our day.

> **"Love...It does not demand its own way. It is not irritable, and it keeps no record of being wronged." - 1 Corinthians 13:5 NLT**

We can't control if the day (or night) goes our way, but we can choose whether or not it steals our joy. We can choose how we respond and react to it. So that morning, despite our exhaustion, despite wanting to crawl back into bed, we chose to change the narrative. We went out for a walk and got some fresh air and sunshine. We walked to the nearest Starbucks and got some coffee. We listened to worship music and let the girls run around the trail and park, and enjoyed our time as a family.

And guess what? It completely shifted our moods and was such a beautiful start to our day. I felt less tired afterward, and felt more connected to my family and filled with joy.

Whether you're a parent or not, we all have those days. The days where we wake up on the "wrong side of the bed" and wish we could crawl into a hole somewhere. We're tired, and our fuse is short.

What I've observed is that our moods are often contagious. Whether it is your home or your workplace: *we impact the people around us with our attitudes.* The good news is that as hard as it is sometimes, we are powerful to shift our moods and change the atmosphere.

Sometimes we just need to stop and take a moment to recalibrate; to adjust our attitude and our perspective. To pause, breathe, and choose joy. To take a minute to invite God's patience and peace into our hearts and minds. Where we fall short, **He** is our strength. He strengthens us with the power of the Holy Spirit, giving us patience and endurance.

"Being strengthened with all power according to His glorious might so that you may have great endurance and patience."
- Colossians 1:11 NIV

I know firsthand how hard it is to snap out of it and adjust my attitude. There are many days when I let my exhaustion and frustration get the best of me, but I also know it is so worth the extra effort to change the narrative! Our emotions and moods can feel so consuming at times, but we have been blessed with a spirit of self-control.

One of the first things I do is to speak life over myself; our thoughts and words have so much power. I try to shift my thinking by declaring, "I'm energized, joyful, and today is going to be a good day." Even if I don't necessarily feel it at the moment, I'd much rather choose that narrative than, "today is the worst. I'm exhausted. My kids are driving me crazy, and nothing is going how I want it to." I have also found power in speaking the verse from Colossians 1:11 (above) over my spirit. It's a matter of simply choosing to speak *life* over yourself and your day, rather than declaring defeat.

"The tongue has the power of life and death, and those who love it will eat its fruit." - Proverbs 18:21 NIV

A few other simple things I do to shift the atmosphere of my home is to make it a point to put on some worship music—worship helps us connect to God and ground ourselves in who He is and whose we are. Singing is a simple way to help you release the frustration you're holding onto and help lift your spirit. I even like to light a candle or diffuse oils, just little things that help me adjust my attitude and therefore shift the atmosphere of my home.

> ## "The LORD is compassionate and gracious,
> ## slow to anger, abounding in love."
> ## - Psalm 103:8 NIV

And remember: If ever you feel like you've failed at this and let another weary day slip by, there is so much grace. His mercies are new every morning… so simply *try try again*.

++++++

Prayer: Lord, thank you that you are my joy. My joy is not found in my circumstances, it is found in you! Help me to release any frustration or irritation I've been holding onto, and to have the strength to change the narrative of my days when I need to. Help me to be slow to anger and abounding in your love, that I might be a light to those around me. Help me to have grace for myself and others, as I partner with you to bring your Kingdom on earth as it is in heaven. In Jesus name, Amen.

Worship Song of the Day: "Build Your Kingdom Here" by Rend Collective, from the album "Campfire."

Response: What helps you to "recalibrate" on the days where you need it? In what ways can you speak life over yourself and your day today? Ask God to fill you up and produce the fruits of the spirit in your life: love, joy, peace, patience, kindness, goodness, faithfulness, gentleness, and self-control (from Galatians 5:22-23 NLT).

_____

_____

_____

_____

_____

DAY SIXTEEN
Rivers In The Wasteland

The last year of my life has been a year of many transitions. I've experienced change, loss, and also with it: *new growth*. In the midst of only a few short months, we moved away from a neighborhood community I adored, my beloved internship ended, and I had to walk away from a ministry and friendship I loved. I found myself grieving all of these losses, experiencing both gratitude for our new home but also feelings of loneliness and isolation in the transition. I felt so distant from all the community and friendship I had worked so hard to build.

It felt like the rug was pulled out from underneath me. My heart and emotions felt so raw and vulnerable. I cried out to God with so many questions and so much heartache. How could I, in the blink of an eye, go from a such a fruitful, thriving season, straight into the wilderness?

The thing about the wilderness though, is that you are suddenly face to face with God. It is just you and Him, as you cry out to Him and allow Him to slowly heal your broken heart. I pursued Him every day because I needed His strength to carry me through. In my prayers, He whispered to my heart, "you are in the season of Fall, the old is falling away as I prepare to do a new thing, but hold steadfast, because **Spring is coming.**"

Spring is coming. I held on so tightly to those words, to that promise from Him. It carried me through the emptiness and the loneliness of that season. Though I felt isolated and rejected at times, I held on tightly to the truth: God never has and never will leave me or reject me.

> "For I am about to do something new. See,
> I have already begun! Do you not see it?
> I will make a pathway through the wilder-
> ness. I will create rivers in the dry waste-
> land." - Isaiah 43:19 NLT

I tear up as I write out that scripture above because God was so **faithful** throughout that season. He held me close as I held tightly back onto Him, in full dependence. In my weakness, He was strong. He was faithful to make a pathway through the wilderness and rivers in the wasteland; showing me His goodness and mercy all along the way!

> "Don't be afraid, for I am with you. Don't
> be discouraged, for I am your God. I will
> strengthen you and help you. I will hold you
> up with my victorious right hand."
> - Isaiah 41:10 NLT

It is so important that we draw close to God, allowing His love to fill every crack and crevice in our hearts; to fill ourselves with His truth and love and grace in **every season.** That way, in seasons where you feel dry and barren, you have reserves of His love within you to draw from.

++++++

Prayer: Lord, thank you that you are doing a new thing in me. Help me not to be discouraged, but to trust that you are making a way for me. Thank you that you never leave, you are right there in every season and every storm. Help me to hold tightly to you and your truth, and fill me up with your presence. Turn my bitter into sweet, and my winter into spring. In Jesus Name, Amen.

Worship Song of The Day: "Bitter/Sweet" by Amanda Cook, from the album "Brave New World."

Response: What is your current season like? Ask God to speak to your heart about what season you're in, and give you something to hold onto. Write down any new growth you'd like to see happen in your life and ask Him for ways to cultivate that growth.

_____

_____

_____

_____

DAY SEVENTEEN
"Should-ing" On Yourself

I should read my bible more.

I should pray more.

I should get up earlier.

I should exercise more.

I should lose weight.

I should be more generous.

I should be more organized.

I should steward my time and talents better.

I should stop getting on social media.

I should really floss.

I should be more neighborly.

I should be more selfless.

I should not have said that.

I should be more patient.

I should cook more.

I should go to bed earlier.

I should stop procrastinating.

I should clean my house more.

And the list goes *on and on and on.*

That awkward moment when you realize you've been "should-ing" all over yourself. It starts so easily, a couple "shoulds" here and there... and before you know it, your mind is overtaken by a laundry list of self-imposed expectations. None of which you can ever meet, at least not all at once, and when the expectations are not met you slowly begin to feel like you've failed miserably.

And so the insecurities begin to creep in. These insecurities can often lead to comparison; assuming everyone else is somehow succeeding at all of these things except you.

I'm not saying it is bad to have goals or things you are working on; I am all for personal growth! But I do think a little reflection on what is driving it is sometimes necessary. Is it driven by fear? By anxiety that says you're not enough or not doing enough? By a need to earn acceptance and approval from others or yourself?

Sometimes we have to do a little searching of our hearts and take time to pray and surrender these things before our "shoulds" create unnecessary stress and anxiety that only lead to defeat.

In these moments, I sneak away, whenever and however I can, to spend time alone with God. Not because I "should," but because I genuinely desire to rest with my Jesus. I allow myself time to soak in His presence without pressure or expectation, enjoying the opportunity to **be still.**

"Be still, and know that I am God."
- Psalm 46:10 NIV

God is always faithful to meet me there and fill me with His transcendent peace. Not because I've earned it or proven my worth or somehow impressed Him, but because **I am His daughter.** He sees so much beauty and worth and value in me; even when I don't always see it in myself.

I think at their root our "shoulds" can stem from judgment and self-criticism. Judgment that we are not doing the "right" things, not doing our best, not living how we "should." So often we are our harshest critics. And then there's the shame. Shame about our failures, our inadequacies, areas we feel we're not measuring up.

In these moments, we can look to **Him.** We can lay aside our judgments, and invite His love into the deepest and darkest parts of our hearts— allowing Him to heal us from the inside out. We can cast our fear and anxiety on Him and trust that He is strong enough to carry the weight of it.

> **"I sought the Lord, and he answered me; he delivered me from all my fears. Those who look to him are radiant; their faces are never covered with shame."**
> **- Psalm 34:4-5 NIV**

Look to Him, and He will deliver you from your fears and take away your shame. Let go of anything not of Him, so you can step into all that He created you to be.

You are radiant. You are loved. You are worthy.

++++++

Prayer: Lord, thank you that I can be still in your presence. Help my heart not to be burdened by all the things I "should do" and focus instead on who you created me to be. I pray that I would not be anxious or obsessed with trivial things, but have the strength to keep my gaze transfixed on you alone! I release my self-criticism and judgment and pray that you will help me to love myself as you do. Thank you that you are always with me, help me to be aware of your presence today. In Jesus Name, Amen.

Worship Song of the Day: "God I Look To You (Live)" by Bethel Music & Francesca Battistelli, from the album "Starlight (Live)"

Response: Do you ever find yourself overloaded with all the things you "should" do? Do you find yourself feeling like you've fallen short of your self-imposed expectations? Write your own list of "shoulds" to release and let go. If you struggle with anxiety or panic attacks, put your hand over your heart and declare, "peace, be still, in Jesus name." Use this declaration any time anxiety creeps in.

DAY EIGHTEEN
Spring Cleaning

I am what my husband lovingly calls a "surface cleaner." I tidy the house, so everything is neat and orderly and presentable, but never seem to do the deep cleaning. You know, the down-on-your-hands-and-knees scrubbing and polishing. The stuff that usually goes unnoticed.

This may be the state of my home, but I sure hope it's not the state of my heart and mind. I want to do the Spring cleaning of my soul so that things do not just look pretty and presentable on the surface, but that deep-down, where no one sees, I have a pure heart. A tender, responsive heart that is full of God's grace and love.

> "Create in me a pure heart, O God, and renew a steadfast spirit within me."
> - Psalm 51:10 NIV

God has given us a new heart and a new spirit, like Christ. But sometimes old patterns and habits can keep us from living as the new creation that we are. If we don't take occasional inventory and clean out the old cobwebs in our hearts and minds; we will slowly begin to feel distant from God.

> "I will give you a new heart and put a new spirit in you; I will remove from you your heart of stone and give you a heart of flesh." - Ezekiel 36:26 NIV

As we stay close to God and allow His spirit to live in us and through us, we can rid ourselves of those habits that can lead to long-term self-destruction; habits that, over time, can wear down your spirit and leave you feeling empty, isolated, and at your breaking point.

We have the power to lay down our unhealthy habits and behaviors, and choose a new way; a way that leads towards life, and life to the full.

Here are some questions I like to reflect on to clean out my mind and purify my heart so that I can walk in freedom. These are usually the three patterns of behavior that I, like many others, slip into when I'm distracted, anxious, or disconnected from God. I let the self-awareness lead me to prayer and confession so that I can recalibrate and cleanse my heart and mind, reconnecting my heart to **His.**

1. Am I seeking approval and validation from others?

It's so enticing, isn't it? Praise and validation from others feels good. Finding our validation and self-worth based on what others think or say about us only feeds our insecurities. It becomes habitual, becomes ingrained in our minds.

In the end, it leaves us feeling empty, unworthy, and like we don't measure up.

What if instead of finding our worth from others, we found our worth in who God says we are? Worth and value are determined by what someone is willing to pay, and Jesus paid the highest price for us. **This kind of worth does not change based on other people's opinions: it is steadfast, never changing, never ending.** We can come to Him and find our validation in who He is, who He says we are, and His great love for us.

> "Then Christ will make his home in your hearts as you trust in him. Your roots will grow down into God's love and keep you strong. " - Ephesians 3:17-21 NLT

So, whenever you feel yourself slowly sinking into unhealthy habits of people pleasing, approval seeking, or in need of validation— remind yourself that your identity and worth are found in Him, and grow roots deep down into His love.

2. Am I letting my worry consume me?

We've all had those moments. A worrisome thought or circumstance pops into our minds, and before we know it our thoughts are spiraling out of control, and we feel anxious. When our minds are filled with anxious thoughts about the future, it distracts us from focusing on what God is doing right now. Choosing not to live in worry doesn't necessarily mean everything will go our way, it means we are choosing to trust God's faithfulness and provision in our lives regardless of our circumstances. We can be careless in HIS care and choose not partner with worry, fear, and anxiety.

> "Give your entire attention to what God is doing right now, and don't get worked up about what may or may not happen tomorrow. God will help you deal with whatever hard things come up when the time comes."
> - Matthew 6:34 MSG

We must search our minds and release anything that is troubling us so that we can receive His peace.

3. Am I engaging in negative self-talk or believing lies about who I am?

We've all experienced our inner critic. The voice that tells us we're not good enough. The little lies whispering to us that we're fat, stupid, unworthy, unlovable, or a failure. For many years negative self-talk overwhelmed my thoughts. I was so critical of myself, belittling myself in my mind and not believing the truth of who God says I am. It was easier to believe the lies of the enemy than the reality of what God says.

The enemy of our souls whispers lies in our ears, and the problem is that we listen, and worse— we agree. And this excessive self-criticism has been linked to anxiety and depression. The enemy has us right where He wants us. It's a vicious cycle, but it is one we can **intentionally** choose to break.

We need to silence this critic. It does not bring life, but destruction. We can choose to break agreement with what He says about us and believe who God says we are: fearfully and wonderfully made in His image.

How do we silence it? We take **every thought captive** and make it submit to Christ. Replace the negative self-talk with the truth, and over time this will renew your mind and break the habit.

> "We demolish arguments and every pretension that sets itself up against the knowledge of God, and we take captive every thought to make it obedient to Christ"
> - 2 Corinthians 10:5 NIV.

On the next page I've listed some common lies we often believe, that we can take captive and replace with God's truth. As we continually take these thoughts captive, and declare the truth, we can transform and renew our minds.

LIE	TRUTH
I am a failure	I am victorious [Romans 8:37]
I am worthless	I am valuable [Matthew 10:31]
I am ugly	I am fearfully & wonderfully made [Psalms 139:13]
I am rejected	I am accepted [Romans 15:7]
I am insignifigant	I am chosen & appointed [John 15: 1, 5]
I am unloved	I am loved by God [Romans 5:8]
I am guilty	I have been forgiven & redeemed [Ephesians 1:7]
This is impossible	There is nothing God can't do [Jeremiah 32:27]
This will never end	This is but a temporary season [2 Corinthians 4:18]

You are **chosen**. You are **loved**. You are **seen** and **known** by a loving, gracious Father. Let us walk in that victorious truth today.

++++++

Prayer: Lord, thank you for your grace and power. Search my heart and purify me, so that I can walk in the fullness of your love. Thank you that I am victorious in Christ— Help me walk in victory today and every day. I renounce all the lies that I have believed about myself and choose to partner with your truth and who you say I am. In Jesus name, Amen.

Worship Song of the Day: "Break Every Chain (Live)" by Tasha Cobbs Leonard, from the album "Grace."

Response: Do you ever fall into any of these patterns/habits? Confess anything that may be heavy on your heart. If there are any lies you've believed about yourself, take time to identify them and declare the truth. Write them down and try to memorize the truth and the coordinating scripture.

_____

_____

_____

_____

_____

_____

DAY NINETEEN
From Rejected To Accepted

It started off like any other morning. I was massively pregnant with my second daughter and was rushing out the door in the morning to get to my women's bible study. I was running late, yet again, and to be honest— I almost didn't even go. But I pressed on, feeling like I was supposed to be there.

That day, we had been reading and discussing how God gives us new names. He changes our names to establish our new identities or to call out what will happen in our lives. In Genesis 17, He changes Abram's name to Abraham, meaning "father of a multitude" and He changes Sarai's name to Sarah, meaning "mother of nations." In the New Testament, we see Jesus changing Simon's name to Peter, meaning "rock." Just as God was speaking to them about their new identity, so too does He speak to us and gives us new names. So this day, they asked us to pray and ask God what our new name was. I closed my eyes to pray, but I still felt off, and I didn't expect to hear anything. But immediately, unexpectedly, God brought forth a memory to my mind. A memory I had long since forgotten.

It was me, when I was only nine years old, overhearing my Father talk to His girlfriend at the time about me. He was telling her that I was always my mom's black sheep of the family; that I was her least favorite of her six children. God spoke to my spirit and told me that day I had partnered with the lie that I was rejected, but that He has changed my name from **rejected** to **accepted**.

Tears streamed down my face as I received this word and realized how true it was, and how much this spirit of rejection had affected my life. I had been deeply insecure, desperate to be liked and validated by others. I needed healing so that I could break that lie of rejection and believe in my true identity as an accepted child of God.

> "But you are the ones chosen by God,
> chosen for the high calling of priestly work,
> chosen to be a holy people, God's instru-
> ments to do his work and speak out for him,
> to tell others of the night-and-day difference
> he made for you— from nothing to some-
> thing, from rejected to accepted."
> - 1 Peter 2: 9-10 MSG

I couldn't help but be in awe of His goodness and faithfulness that day! He showed up— revealing a part of myself that I didn't even know about, a moment from my past that I did not remember so that I could find healing and freedom! I left that day feeling as though the fog that I had been seeing through had lifted, as I embraced my new name: **accepted**.

We were not created to live in bondage. God's heart is for us to find **freedom**, on earth as it is in heaven.

It was God's heart for me to find healing that day. He didn't want me to live with the fear of rejection, He wanted me to break free so that I could live loved and whole.

> "Now the Lord is the Spirit, and where the Spirit of the Lord is, there is freedom. And we all, who with unveiled faces contemplate the Lord's glory, are being transformed into his image with ever-increasing glory, which comes from the Lord, who is the Spirit."
> - 2 Corinthians 3:17-18 NIV

++++++

Prayer: Lord, I praise you for your faithfulness! Thank you that you have redeemed me— from nothing to something, from rejected to accepted. Thank you that you are transforming me to be more like you. Reveal anything in my life that may be enslaving me, so that I can walk in complete freedom. In Jesus name, Amen.

Worship Song of the Day: "Freedom Reigns" by Jesus Culture (featuring Kim Walker-Smith), from the album "Come Away (Live)."

Response: Take some time to pray and ask God what your new name is. Write down what you hear. Ask God to bring forth any memories or areas of pain that may be enslaving you, and invite His Holy Spirit to bring restoration and healing.

_____

_____

_____

_____

_____

_____

DAY TWENTY
Not In A Hurry

There I was. Frantic. Rushing. The picture of "desperate housewife" with my messy mom-bun and yoga pants (it's a stigma because it's true). My day was filled with errands and obligations and crossing off to-do lists. I would like to say I handle such days with elegance and grace, but that would just be untrue. I was exhausted and my fuse was short. And try as I might to be on time to something, I always seem to fail. And when errands that should take 45 minutes end up taking three hours with my kids in tow, my patience starts to wear thin. And it leaves me exhausted. The kind of exhausted that you feel in your bones. And just, *why?* Why does it all feel so hard and overwhelming some days?

The thing is, as I pause long enough to reflect on this constant state of rushing, I realize it is not just circumstantial: it's **spiritual.** Something inside that feels it needs to *hurry and rush and "keep up."* As if I'm at risk of being left behind otherwise. As if I'm not enough as I am: I'm not accomplishing enough, not working hard enough, not productive enough. I'm always looking ahead to what is next instead of focusing on the present moment.

And what God has been teaching me this last year is how to *slow down.* How to rest in Him. How to lay down my burdens and anxieties and trust in Him. I don't have to go it alone anymore— **He's with me.** And when I lean on Him, He fills me with the supernatural peace of the Holy Spirit. So that even in the midst of all the chaos of this season, with its many trials and daily battles, I can be at rest. Not rushing. Not striving. Just being.

> **"Slow down. Take a deep breath. What's the hurry? Why wear yourself out? Just what are you after anyway?"** - Jeremiah 2:25 MSG

Every morning I take time to invite God into my day. I want to partner with Him to get through it. I want to give Him the first fruits of my time so that I can walk into my day, whatever is in store, from a place of rest and love. Even on my busiest days, taking time for a simple prayer of surrender can make a huge difference. I used to be "all or nothing" when it came to my time with God. If I didn't have time for a full quiet time and space to be alone to get into the word, I would skip it altogether. And let's be honest, that's not always a reality when you have little ones or a busy schedule! Now I know that God wants to be with me in each moment of my day, and I can invite Him into every part. Sometimes my most powerful times of prayer are in the kitchen making breakfast for the kids or while I'm in the shower or doing laundry. Of course, I still love to set aside time whenever I can to be with Him, but when that's not a reality, I still seek Him. And that helps me to stay connected and grounded in Him: to hear His voice and not just merely rush from one thing to the next.

> **"Quiet down before God, be prayerful before him. Don't bother with those who climb the**

ladder, who elbow their way to the top."
- Psalm 37:7 MSG

God designed us for a relationship with Him, and He's always drawing us closer to Him. Let's not be so busy and distracted that we miss it and miss out on the depths of intimacy that He has for us. He wants to come in and fill us up, to be our place of refuge, comfort, and rest. To be the one we open up to and pour our hearts out to. Let's receive His peace and rest, and carry it with us throughout our daily tasks and responsibilities. We don't have to live in a constant state of *hurried frenzy*. We were made for so much more.

++++++

Prayer: Lord, thank you that you designed me for intimacy with you. I pray that I would find rest and refuge in your presence. Help me to slow down and take a deep breath, to breath in your peace and exhale my stress and anxiety. Lord help me to quiet my thoughts and notice when you are speaking. Attune my heart to your presence, and give me ears to hear you and eyes to see you. In Jesus name, Amen.

Worship Song of the Day: "Not In A Hurry" by Will Reagan & United Pursuit, from the album "Tell All My Friends."

Response: Do you ever feel like you are rushing through life? Or struggle to take time to rest in God's presence? Take a minute to pour your heart out to God. Tell Him if anything is worrying you or creating anxiety in you. Then take a few minutes to pray and meditate on the verse "be still and know that I am God" from Psalm 46:10.

_____

_____

_____

_____

_____

_____

FINAL THOUGHTS

Almost two years ago I was standing in my bedroom when I felt God speak to me and tell me the names of books/devotionals I would someday write. I almost chuckled at Him, because that felt so far from the reality I was living. One of the names He gave me was **Draw Near**. I wrote it down in my journal and left it at that for the time being.

The idea would occasionally pop in and out of my mind for a few years, but the timing never felt right. And then, suddenly, one day as I was walking and praying...

God said, *"Now. Write Draw Near now."*

I went home that day with a flood of inspiration, as the words and ideas came pouring out of me. I set a deadline, but I ended up reaching my goal in half the time. When God is in it, there is nothing you cannot do. He will equip you with the inspiration, the creativity, the words, the prayers, the resources-- whatever it is you need to fulfill His call. When we work in partnership with Him, incredible things begin to happen!

I pray that this book has encouraged you and drawn you closer to the very heart of God. Every good thing that has happened in my life has been birthed out of my intimate relationship with Him. I pray that you would fall in love with Him *over and over and over again* as you discover new depths of His **goodness, mercy, and love!**

From My Heart To Yours,

Monika

++++++

SPECIAL THANKS

Thank you, Jesus, for your love that changed *everything*.

Thank you to my incredible husband, Ryan, I seriously don't know what I'd do without you! I am so grateful for all the late nights you spent designing my cover and layout, and for all the insight and encouragement you provided along the way. You are truly the most talented, incredible, and hilarious human I've ever met. And you're mine!

Thank you to Bianca Olthoff and the incredible team I interned with at *In The Name of Love*. That summer changed my life. I will never forget it, or any of you. Soul sisters forever.

Thank you to my Pastor, Todd Rodarmel, and my church family at Mountain View Church in San Juan Capistrano. The last seven years have been the most transformative years of my life, and I am forever grateful. Thank you for showing me that the restoration of all things is, indeed, possible.

Thank you to all of the friends and family members who have spoken life over me, encouraged me, believed in me, and loved me along the way. You make my life richer and more meaningful in every way possible.

And finally, thank you to **you,** *whoever and wherever you are,* for reading this and for having the courage and faith to pursue a deeper relationship with Jesus.

STAY CONNECTED

 WEBSITE monikakirkland.com

 FACEBOOK Monika Kirkland

 INSTAGRAM @monikakirkland

 EMAIL hello@monikakirkland.com

REQUEST MONIKA TO SPEAK

For retreats, conferences, one-night gatherings, church services, leadership events.

NOTES

Made in the USA
San Bernardino, CA
17 September 2018